The Floating Markets of Bangkok

Written by
Cath Jones

This is Bangkok. It is big and bright.

But we are not staying in Bangkok. We are travelling south west, to visit a floating market.

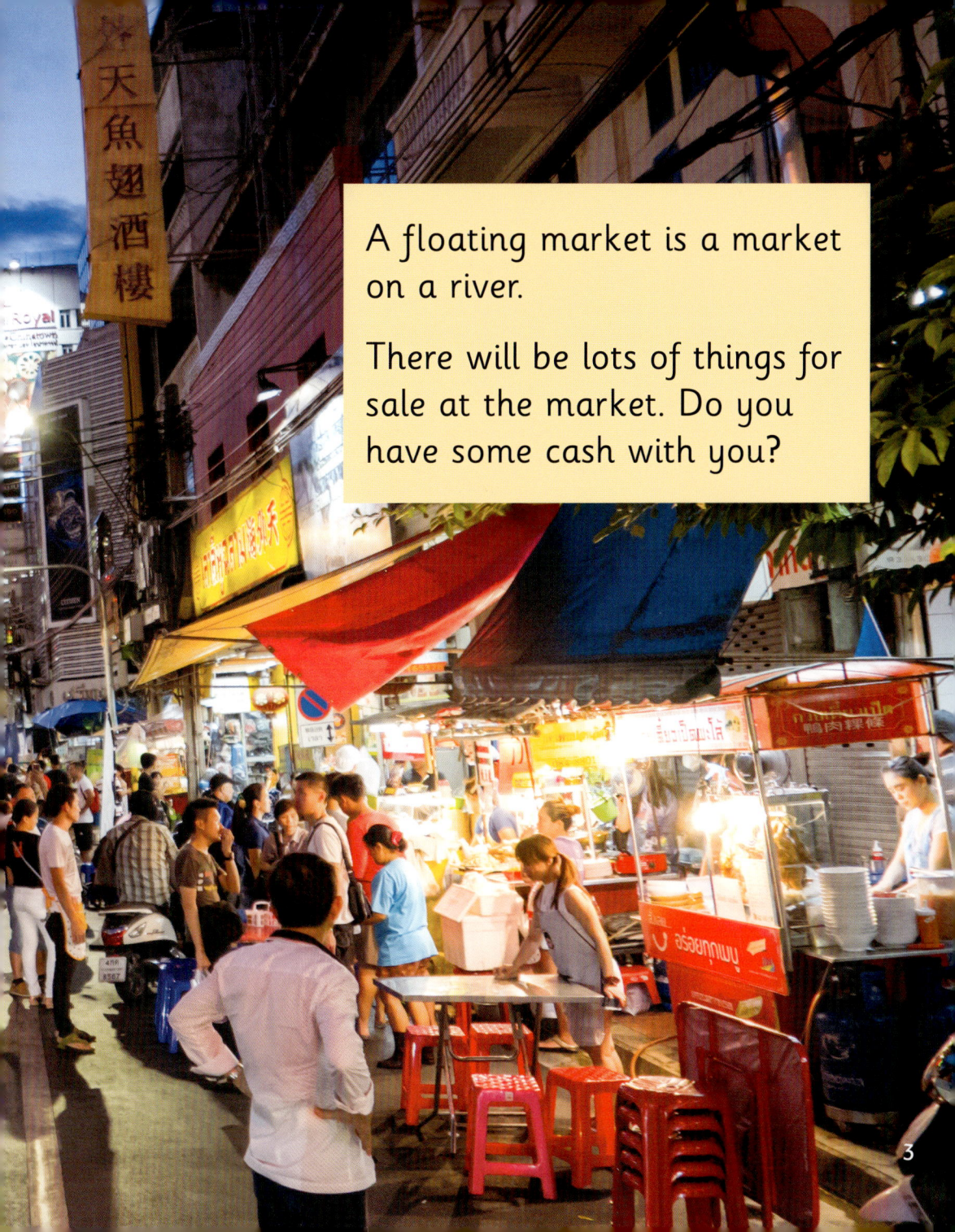

A floating market is a market on a river.

There will be lots of things for sale at the market. Do you have some cash with you?

Come on, it's time to go.

This is called a **tuk tuk**. People in Bangkok often travel in these.

Jump in! We will ride to the market in this tuk tuk.

The market is on the river. There are lots of boats.

The boats glide on the river until they reach the market. Look at them bobbing up and down. We must not be late!

What an astonishing sight! There are such a lot of boats.

It looks like a colossal traffic jam, but it's a traffic jam made of boats!

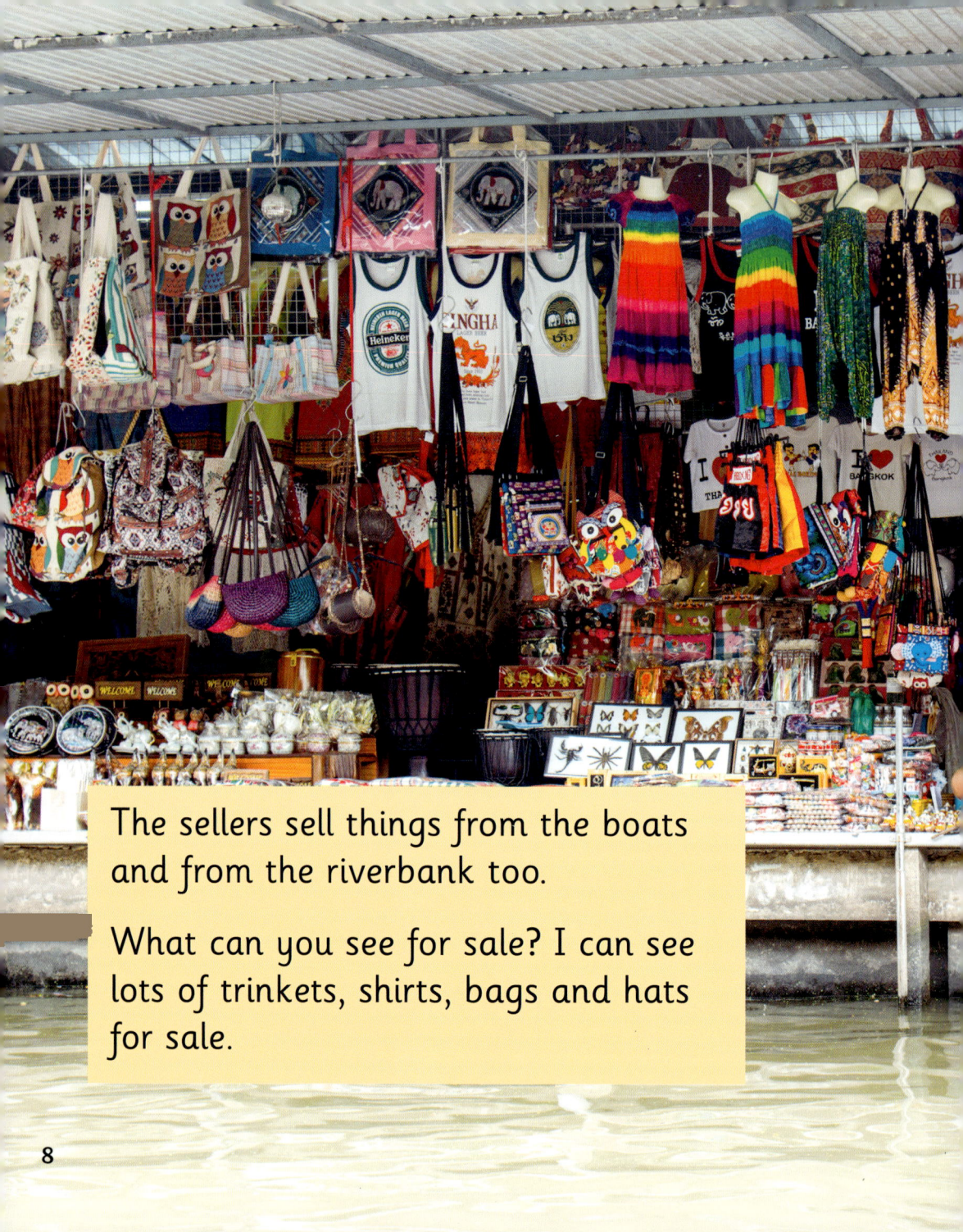

The sellers sell things from the boats and from the riverbank too.

What can you see for sale? I can see lots of trinkets, shirts, bags and hats for sale.

You can see snakes at the market too, but they are not for sale!

You can get food at the market too. Look at all the things to eat. It is all so fresh!

There are orchards and farmland close to the market. The sellers harvest the food when it is ripe. Then they take it to the market to sell.

Do you like street food?

You can get hot food at the market. People will cook it on the boats, just for you!

Look, she is cooking on this boat.

Some sellers are grilling meat. Some sellers are cooking seafood. Is it fried, or is it steamed?

The sun shines all day, so how do people stay cool? Those wide-brimmed hats do a good job! They keep you in the shade.

Look, she has a fan.
She waves it to stay cool.

Are you glad you came down the river to see the floating market?

Did it amaze you? Did you enjoy it? I hope so.

See you next time!